Lost and Found
Copyright © 2015 by Liza Finlay

Liza Finlay
5 Ravina Crescent
Toronto, ON, Canada M4J 3L09

Phone: 416-807-0979
Email: lizafinlay@rogers.com
Website: www.lizafinlay.com

ISBN 978-0-9893354-2-3

Dedication

For Diana Donald, who showed me the way.

Acknowledgements

A big thank you to all "the ladies"—the sisterhood
of women who encouraged, read and re-read: Leah
Macpherson, Jasmine Miller, Fina Scroppo and Alyson
Schafer. Heartfelt gratitude to the mentors who went before
me and lead the charge: Carole Finlay, Jean Tully and
Marina Bluvshtein. To my spouse Chris, who cheered me
on, no matter what. And to all the beautiful clients who
trusted me with their stories.

The Spiritual Journey
of Women at Midlife

By Liza Finlay

Introduction

Alone on an Endless Sea

"Midway upon the journey of our life I found myself within a forest dark, for the straightforward pathway had been lost."
— Dante Alighieri

I remember it being a cloudless summer day—the sun was hot and the sky infinite. Under that endless expanse of blue, the lake stretched out beneath the bow of my boat with equally infinite possibility. I was at the halfway point: Looking back, I could see the cottage peeking through the birch on the point; ahead lay the rocky outcropping that was my destination. Or rather, the outcropping that should have been my destination. Yet there I was, midway through my journey, drifting. I could keep paddling. I could "motor" on. I just didn't want to. The trouble was, I didn't know where else to go. I didn't know where to point the bow of my boat. So I just sat there, bobbing up and down with the waves and going nowhere.

Now, I'd love to be able to tell you how—perched in my boat with paddle in hand—I felt the potent exhilaration that comes with endless possibility. Or, at the very least, I'd like to be able to tell you how, in monk-like manner, I embraced the Zen of the moment and sat in in serene silence, in utter enjoyment of the moment.

Well, neither of those things happened. (And that's a good thing, too, because without some kind of major emotional turning point we wouldn't have much of a book.) Instead, I wept. I cried so hard I worried that I might have to start baling out the boat. "What is wrong with me?" I asked myself. There was no imminent threat. There were no storm clouds looming. I was in no danger of capsizing or drowning.

I was lost.

Floating aimlessly on that lake I was struck by the realization that my life felt just as aimless as this aquatic diversion. At the midway point of my life, I found myself in the doldrums. Looking back I could see a trail of accomplishments culminating in career, kids, happy coupledom. But looking ahead? Well, I just couldn't fathom the next two decades being a repeat performance of the last two. Doing so left me with a deep sense of dread. I couldn't keep going in the same direction. But what was the alternative? The path forward wasn't clear and that left me with a profound sense of emptiness, of being directionless. I was drowning and searching for a lifeline. I was grasping for something, but for precisely what I couldn't tell.

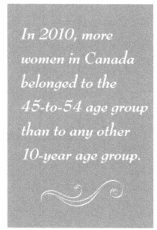

In 2010, more women in Canada belonged to the 45-to-54 age group than to any other 10-year age group.

Eventually I figured it out. After donning and discarding a dozen or so solutions I found the fix that fit. At 40, I reinvented myself. Or, perhaps more aptly, I rediscovered myself. After looking under all the nooks and crannies of my life, I found parts of myself that I'd lost along the way. And, after enduring months floating aimlessly—lost in my own life—I found new purpose. I found new direction. I found myself. Again.

At midlife, I went back to school, earned a graduate degree in counselling psychology and became a psychotherapist. I specialize in adolescents and midlife women, which is not as incongruous a pairing as you might think. In many ways, midlife is like a second adolescence—both life stages are characterized by feelings of being lost, by a yearning to feel true belonging, to feel a true fit. Both populations are struggling with identity issues; while teens are trying to find themselves, women at midlife are trying to find themselves again. If teens are inventing themselves, midlife women are re-inventing themselves.

Today, middle-aged women account for the fastest-growing segment of overdose deaths in the United States; the Centers for Disease Control and Prevention reports a boom in prescription-drug use among women at midlife, and points to skyrocketing prescription-drug deaths among this population.

Today, many of the souls I serve are women just like me. The story of being lost and found at midlife isn't mine alone. It belongs to all of us. At the midpoint of life, many women feel adrift. Rudderless. Lost. Once certain of where she was going, a woman at midlife finds herself faltering. By all appearances she has it all—a family, financial stability, a future. So why do she feel so forlorn?

A 2011 Gallup-Healthways Well-Being Index revealed that women aged 45 to 64 have the lowest well-being of any age group or gender.

In short, many midlife women have lost track of what it takes to be truly happy in this chapter of their lives. They have lost touch with who they really are in this phase of their evolution. It isn't that their past lives have been a charade, only that the part they played no longer fits.

And that leaves millions of North American middle-aged women at a crucial turning point—immersed in the mire of what I call "**midlife malaise**." It's like someone has hit the dimmer switch. Life isn't black, so much as grey. They don't feel depressed but rather despondent. It's as if joy has decamped and they can't find its hiding place.

A 2010 Gallup poll reported that nearly two-thirds of middle-aged North American women drink alcohol regularly, a number higher than at any time in the past 25 years.

Finding that joy isn't just optimal, it's essential to mental and emotional health. The revolutionary psychological theorist Carl Jung even went so far as to suggest that while the first half of life is about turning outward, the second half is about turning inward—it's about nurturing authenticity, courage and wisdom. This coming to terms with self and finding a way to live congruently with that self is the primary task of midlife. It's the next stage of our evolution—as women, as human beings.

Building upon my own experience, and that of the many female clients I've helped navigate this dark passageway, I've created a roadmap to help readers find their way through midlife malaise and into a brighter future. So let's get started. Your journey awaits.

$\mathcal{S}$ummary of Key Points:

- Feeling lost is common for women at midlife; "midlife malaise" is a universal feeling. Navigating the midlife transition is a crucial developmental stage and one that reaps myriad spiritual rewards.

- The key to answering the call of midlife is to turn inward. Most pundits and psychological theorists agree that the second half of life is about focusing on our inner, emotional landscape.

- The primary task at midlife is coming to terms with one's self—the person we are now, not the person we think we should be, and not the person tied to prescribed roles and duties.

- Numerous studies confirm that becoming "found" is essential to both mental and emotional health.

Notes:

Chapter 1

Reorientation:
Finding Your Embarkation Point

"If my ship sails from sight, it doesn't mean my journey ends, it simply means the river bends."

— Enoch Powell

Midlife has traditionally been treated with mockery. Jokes about the "midlife crisis" abound and in Hollywood this era is cast as one in which men have affairs, buy expensive bespoke suits and even more expensive sports cars. And the women? They just drive off the deep end. Frazzled, frumpy, harebrained and hellish to live with—this is how middle-aged women are portrayed in television and movies.

Indeed, a 2010 study of 13 American films revealed that the midlife woman's body is more frequently viewed as an object of humour versus an object of desire.

What popular culture fails to address are the strengths unique to this stage of life. And maybe that's because we've all lost sight of them. So, if we are going to make it across this great divide we **need a change of attitude.**

A 2014 study found that women with a prior history of depression or anxiety were vulnerable to a recurrence of depression at the midlife transition.

We need to build a new consciousness—a renaissance consciousness. We need to reorient ourselves, to stop looking back and start looking ahead. We need to do what psychotherapists call a "reframe." We aren't ending a chapter, we are beginning a fresh one. We aren't mourning failed dreams, we are creating new ones. These are the labour pains that signify rebirth. This is the feeling of being "lost" that comes before you are found.

Suzanne Braun Levine, the first editor of *Ms. Magazine* and author of *Inventing the Rest of Our Lives*, describes midlife as a "fertile void" —an abyss (albeit a fertile one) yawning between what was and what is yet to come. I prefer to think of this stage as a fertile valley. Behind us are the great heights we've scaled—the house we bought, the kids we raised (or are raising), the jobs we've had, the financial ups and downs. Ahead of us are mountains we've yet to climb. In the middle is the somewhat dark, shaded, yet richly silted valley through which we need to travel to get to those next heights. There is no question that travelling through this valley will tire us, but it is equally without question that this fertile passage will reap great rewards. This is a valley rife with opportunity.

That doesn't make it easy. What epic voyage ever is? I liken the feeling of being lost to a state of limbo. No one likes limbo—it's dreary, energy-less, soul sucking. What I'm asking you to do is settle in and get comfortable there—just for a bit. Don't fight it. Instead, invite those lost, listless feelings in and ask them to have a seat. You've got a few questions you'd like to ask.

A book on midlife women published by the National Association of Social Workers (in America) reported that nearly half of women age 51 appraise their lives as first rate. These women experienced a high sense of personal achievement and a new sense of adventure.

You can't possibly know which direction you want your life to go in, what shape you want it to take, until you know what's missing from it in the here and now. As we move through this book, I'll give you some insights to help you make sense of your feelings and some strategies to help you put them to best use. But for now, step one of this marvelous midlife journey is to put down those defenses—the judging, avoiding, downplaying, excuse-making. Therapists specialized in Adlerian psychology, as I am, call these "safeguarding strategies"—they are designed to guard against feelings of inferiority, against feelings we are uncomfortable facing.

"There must be something wrong with me if I'm feeling this way."

"I have no right to be unhappy."

"If I were a better/smarter person I'd be happy."

"It's not me—it's the state of the world."

"It's just a stage—it will go away."

Yes, what you're going through is hard, but if you take the time to honour your feelings and not judge or shy away from them you'll be all the better on the other side.

Typically, before you embark on a journey you pack your bags. For this journey, step one requires you to unpack your bags and stay awhile. I want you to lean into that lost feeling instead of pulling away. I want you to change the lens through which you view this emotional state. Put away those dim, dark glasses and

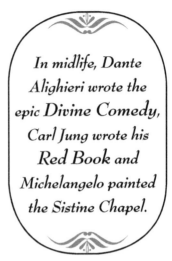

In midlife, Dante Alighieri wrote the epic Divine Comedy, Carl Jung wrote his Red Book and Michelangelo painted the Sistine Chapel.

pick up a magnifying glass. It's time to play detective. Your feelings are clues; they provide you with invaluable data. That data help you map out the changes you'll need to make in your life.

Journaling

What you *feel* is the best way to determine what you *need*. Take some time to explore, and journal, the following...

I am feeling (use as many adjectives as possible)_____

_____

I began to feel this way (when? where? with whom?)_____

_____

My feelings are most pronounced when_____

I tend to feel better after I/when I _____

I feel the most joy when I _____

On a scale of 1 to 10 (10 being most positive), I rank my love life: ___

On a scale of 1 to 10 (10 being most positive), I rank my friendships: ___

On a scale of 1 to 10 (10 being most positive), I rank my work life: ___

On a scale of 1 to 10 (10 being most positive), I rank my self-worth: ___

Redefining Worth

If midlife malaise is characterized by the feeling of being untethered, it's because all the things that once defined our self-worth now seem of questionable value. The things that once seemed important no longer do. And that's a good thing. Sure, feeling anchorless and adrift is pretty scary, but where you're headed the waters are deeper and more clear.

Most people have spent their lives amassing self-worth like they would tabulate columns in a profit and loss statement. It's a point system, with what you do and what you have being tallied up on a psychic ledger sheet. In the end, your self-worth comes down to an appraisal of all you've accumulated. Get a promotion, do a good deed, renovate the garage—these go on the plus side of the ledger. Get passed over for a promotion, fight with your kids, forget your brother's birthday—these get stacked against you. Your self-esteem goes up and down like the stock market and, like the stock market, you've had some good runs. It's an approach that's been OK. Until now.

But, guess what? Your balance sheet just went bust. It's as if at midlife we start to see the futility of this approach. It's only now that we begin to suffer the exhaustion that comes from life on this hamster wheel. With the kids a little less needy and job a little more secure, it's only now, at the midpoint, that we have the luxury to stop and ask ourselves: if not this, then what? It's at midlife—with the kids growing up, the job chugging along—that we have the time and inclination to take a long hard look at our lives and ourselves. It's a mystical moment at the midpoint of our journey when we search for our higher purpose, and for our higher being. It's a time when we ask: What's missing?

Well, I'm here to tell you the part that's missing is you. The "you" that's been showing up for the last two decades isn't enough anymore. It's a shadow self—a version of you that's a little murky and incomplete—that's not quite solid. You now have an opportunity to reconstruct your self-worth using an entirely different model—one that doesn't go up and down based on the opinions of others, one that doesn't sink or swim based on fluctuating performance measures.

Now, let's be clear: I'm not asking you to replace your current measuring stick with a new one. I'm asking you to take the measuring stick, break it across your knees and send it flying.

Instead, I'd like you to build a self-concept based on who you are, not what you do. Doing so will require you to go a little deeper, to unearth the core traits that truly define who you are. These core qualities are yours and yours alone. They are intractable and invulnerable to the changing tide of public opinion and performance appraisals.

In his beautiful book, *The Heart Aroused*, author and poet David Whyte puts it this way: "The road home in some ways is the road back into the body, a time to get to know ourselves again on an interior, almost cellular level. By now, of course, the body into which we journey is middle-aged. It does not respond so well as it used to to the physical demands of the outer world, but its goals can be more humble now, more appropriate to what our hearts know is good and soul-nourishing for us. It has learned how to rest fully into our intuitions and our basic instinctual knowledge of what is right, possible, and useful."

In youth, says Whyte, "our soul's wish for a life and work of our own is tempered by triumph and failure." But with wisdom and age comes a new perspective—one that honours the deeper seat of the soul and connections and contributions that stem from that soul.

And here's the thing: before you can even begin to determine how you need to reconstruct your life, you need to reconstruct your sense of self. You're going to need to tap into your true essence, to rediscover your core traits.

The critical tension we feel in middle age comes from living a life that is increasingly in conflict with our core values. In order to resolve the tension, we need to realign with our values.

So, who are you? Typically, when I ask this question, clients respond with: "I'm an accountant (or professor, or nurse, or mom)." Nope. That's what you do. I want to know who you are. And if you're having trouble answering that question it's because you've spent the last two or three decades losing sight of critical parts of yourself. Doing, more than being. The gift of midlife is the end to that style of existence and the beginning of a richer way of living—one more befitting the older, wiser woman you are.

> *Kendra is a 40-year-old professional with a booming business, a committed partner and three beautiful boys. When her youngest entered Grade 1, Kendra found herself feeling sad almost all the time. "It's as if I just can't figure out how to be happy," she explained. Work and parenting presented constant stress, but Kendra knew that these stresses weren't the real problem. Everywhere she turned, she experienced crippling self-doubt. Interactions with co-workers, neighbours and friends brought up feelings of inadequacy that had been dormant for decades. Everywhere she went she saw a version of herself she wasn't happy with.*

"For years I was able to dismiss these feelings—these moments of self-doubt—but it's like I can't escape them anymore." At 40, with her future stretched out before her, Kendra came face to face with herself. Through therapy, she finally unpacked some baggage that had been weighing her down since childhood, but that she had found ways of dodging or dismissing. Notably, she recalled a traumatic moment when she was five. "I was sick and needed antibiotics. But I was scared to swallow the pill. My dad got mad and shoved the pill down my throat with his fingers. Then he walked away, finished with me. I was humiliated and petrified. At five, I decided that my feelings don't count." Since then, Kendra realized, she had developed a pattern of "swallowing" her feelings (opinions and desires). Instead, she searched for validation from her work performance, her success with friendships and her parenting abilities. "It's like I was measuring my self-worth in every single interaction. I don't do that anymore. I am powerful, strong, wise, adaptable, creative and intuitive—no matter what happens with work, with money, with friends."

Kendra, through a series of therapeutic exercises (some of which you'll find in this chapter), allowed herself to rediscover the core qualities that had been hers since childhood.

The walls of my office are filled with images of trees. That's because, on so many levels, trees are emblematic of the human soul and its journey through life. Branches reach for the sky—though some take twisted and crooked routes—just as we all strive toward a warm, bright future. And, while the tree's branches and leaves appear to show off its unique personality, it's a deeply embedded root system that keeps the tree thriving and growing. As we humans grow through life's stages, we, too, need to dig down deep to find our own root system—the assets, quirks and traits that ground us, define us and allow us to grow.

The Biology of Midlife

Midlife malaise isn't helped by the host of hormonal changes women face as they enter their forties and face perimenopause. Throughout this transition, a woman's estrogen levels rise and fall—along with her weight and, notably, mood.

Many women approaching menopause suffer a sense of detachment from their true selves; it's as if overnight they've been given strange new bodies and temperaments. They often grieve for the physical and emotional beings they once were.

Estrogen loss has led to weight gain, particularly around the middle. It's also contributed to a loss of sexual appetite that leaves many women feeling like they've lost a vital part of themselves. Meanwhile, busy lives (demanding jobs, active families, aging parents) contribute to high levels of cortisol (the stress hormone). It's not uncommon for middle-aged women to experience the cascading effects of chronic stress and depleting estrogen, including insomnia, forgetfulness and mood swings that leave the midlife woman feeling fatigued, irritable and discouraged. "Who am I?" the midlife woman asks herself. Nothing seems to fit anymore. If you were already feeling lost, this doesn't help.

$\mathcal{S}$ummary of Key Points:

- The starting point of a midlife renaissance is a change of attitude; we need to embrace the feelings we experience in order to grow from them. Our labour pains signal rebirth.

- Reframe: you are starting a new chapter, creating new dreams.

- Put aside safeguarding strategies standing between you and your rebirth: excuses, alibis, procrastination.

- "Shoulding" on ourselves prevents us from knowing our true selves and our true desires; it interferes with the spontaneous expression of true selfhood.

- We need to redefine our worth: put aside ways of weighing self-worth based on performance measures, public opinion and the roles we play and renegotiate a sense of self based on who you are at your core.

- Biology plays a crucial role, wreaking havoc on how we look, how we feel and how we feel about ourselves.

The "Should" Mantra

- Take a blank piece of paper and write down all the things you feel you should be doing—for yourself, for others. Don't leave anything out. For example, I should be calling my mother more regularly; I should be having sex more frequently; I should be making more money...

- Tear up the paper. Toss it.

- Get a second blank piece of paper. On it, write the following: "I will stop shoulding on myself!" Post this new mantra somewhere prominent.

23

Strength-Building Visualization

In this exercise, you'll ask your wise, inner self to remind you of all that you are. First, though, you'll need to attune yourself to her. That will require you to get into a state of relaxation.

- Start by sitting in a comfortable position. Feel supported by the chair. Close your eyes and take deep, slow breaths. Focus on each breath as it comes in and goes out. Do this for a few moments. Relax.

- See the inside of your eyes as a blank screen—your third eye. In your mind's eye, take yourself to your favourite place, a place in which you recall being most content, a moment in which you felt most complete. See yourself in that place. Where are you? Who is with you? What are you doing? Is there an animal in this vision? If so, what animal?

- From that place of deep contentment, complete the following sentence: "I am...". Be still, and allow the adjectives to float up into your vision. Don't edit or judge them. This is your highest self speaking.

- Bring yourself back to the room and write down the strengths your truest self revealed to you.

You may want to repeat this exercise often. Every time you do it, new gifts will be revealed.

Strength-Building Interview

Some people have trouble accepting, or believing, their strengths. They need to hear it from someone else. In this exercise, you'll find a trusted friend and ask that friend to honestly answer the following questions:

• What do you feel are the characteristics that make me, me?

• What do I bring to the relationship we share?

• Can you remember a moment in which you felt you benefitted from the real me?

• What is it that you count on me for?

• If I wasn't in your life, what would be missing?

• When you think of me, does a particular colour come to mind? Animal?

Notes:

Notes:

Notes:

Notes:

Chapter 2

Rebirth:
Looking Back to Move Forward

"The childhood shows the man, as morning shows the day."
—John Milton

When I was little, I loved to play doctor. Specifically, I pretended I was a psychologist. I would line up my dolls on the couch and ask them to tell me their problems. Funny huh? As I grew, my path twisted and meandered. I indulged my love of theatre with a brief sojourn on the stage, then I became a magazine writer, started raising a family and finally (yup you've got it, at midlife) I found myself back at school studying to become a psychotherapist.

We knew a lot when we were young. We knew more than we gave ourselves credit for. Mostly, we knew how to be.

We weren't so encumbered by "shoulds"—by self-limiting thoughts and beliefs that interfere with the spontaneous, joyous, easy expression of selfhood. *I might finish last. I might look like an idiot. She might not agree to play with me. It might not work.* When we were children, our doing flowed naturally from our being.

Childhood and adolescence is a rich repository of recollections, many of which help us remember who we are (in a very real, unencumbered state). And childhood isn't just a cache of clues that lead us to our ideal vocation (although almost all my clients have early memories that point them toward their true purpose); connecting to our child-self and adolescent-self can connect us to our lost self.

Jasmine, an architect living in the Midwest, came to see me to talk about her marriage. It wasn't that the marriage was broken down so much as it had a flat tire. It was going nowhere. There was no life in it. In fact, what became clear was that there was no life in Jasmine. She had landed a job in her field—albeit with some challenges—and had two healthy children that she loved. Her partner was committed to doing whatever it took to get their relationship back on track, to make Jasmine happy again. Yet somehow Jasmine couldn't find her happy button. She was constantly skirting sadness, lonely despite being surrounded by her family and peers and lost despite being on a path that was known to her.

Jasmine and I spent a few sessions revisiting Jasmine's childhood. Jasmine had grown up on the ocean, with a yard that backed onto a forest. As a child, she and her friend would lose themselves for hours in that forest, making up games. In one game, they created entire fantasy worlds out of logs, branches, acorns and found objects. "I remember once finding little notes hidden among the leaves in the fairy houses we had created. I learned later that my father had put them there for us to find. He had become an accomplice in our fantasy world."

The word Jasmine used to sum up this childhood memory was "magical." There was a deeply seated sense of enchantment, of fantasy, of whimsy—none of which inhabited her current life. She had grown up and grown away from that magical part of herself. Jasmine's current partner wasn't the sort to turn up the music and start a dance party. She couldn't imagine him hiding notes in the forest for the forest folk her kids had created. "He has little appreciation for spontaneity and silliness." The trouble was, Jasmine didn't just have a tolerance for magical moments, she had a need for them. They were a critical part of who she was at her core.

Jasmine had created a very sensible life for herself. The profession, the partner the children—Jasmine could tick off the boxes on her checklist and feel a sense of accomplishment. But there was one thing missing: her self. Her full self, that is—her silly, nonsensical, capricious, spontaneous, magical self. Somewhere along the way, Jasmine had abandoned parts of herself that were essential to her wholeness. She needed to reclaim those lost parts if she wanted to feel whole again. Moving forward, she needed to find opportunities for magic, for nature, for full-hearted fun. She now knew what was missing from her relationship and from her leisure time.

Which parts of yourself have you lost along the way? Which of those parts are essential to your current wellbeing? Before you can move forward, you need to go back. Midlife is an opportunity to pause and take stock. This is the midway point. You have choices to make about the direction your future takes. Do you keep going the way you've been going? Or do you take a new path? Before you can make that determination, though, you have a bigger question to answer: Who gets to decide? Which version of you? The task in this chapter is to ensure that the person showing up and calling the shots in your life is the you that you truly want showing up for the next couple of decades. Now is your time; this is your moment. Are you full and complete? Are there talents, abilities and passions lying latent in your past that you'd like to go back and retrieve?

The title of this chapter is "Rebirth" for a reason. The gift of midlife is the ability to recreate self, to start again as a more whole, true, complete person. So, before you decide on your future course, figure out what parts of yourself you are content to leave behind and which parts you to need to reclaim.

In the last chapter, we started building a self-concept that was separate from what we do and what we have—and, notably, how others appraise what we do and what we have. In this chapter, we flesh out that self-concept with the missing bits and pieces we've lost along the way. I've included a few exercises to help with that task. Do as many as you can. The more you approach this endeavour with a spirit of curiousity and playfulness, the more fruitful it will be. (This is the fun part, after all.) OK, ready? Get your crayons out.

Summary of Key Points:

- Clues to who we really are and what we really want lie in our childhood. As children, we were not yet so inhibited by self-limiting thoughts and beliefs.

- Before we can go forward we need to go back and retrieve lost parts of ourselves, crucial pieces of our identity that we've abandoned along the way.

- The midway point is an ideal vantage point to stop and take stock—do we keep going along the same path, or take a new path? The direction depends on the person at the steering wheel, the version of you that you choose to let drive.

Give Yourself a Hand

You'll need a blank piece of paper and some coloured pencils or markers for this exercise.

Start by tracing the outline of your hand on the paper. Then, draw or depict the essential parts of yourself in the fingers and on the palm. Find images that represent what's important to you and what defines you. (For example, my "hand" includes a birch tree—because forests are my happy place—and a dragon—representing my fondness for fantasy and magical thinking.)

Remember, this isn't a test of your artistic ability! Rather, this is an opportunity to gain clarity on the various parts of the essential you and the ways in which you have a hand in connecting to the cosmos.

With thanks to the creator of this exercise, Dr. Jill Seibold Sisk, family therapist, author and teacher extraordinaire.

Journal

If you like to write, this is a good one for you. Go treat yourself to a special journal or diary, or use the pages included. Then, without censoring yourself, explore the following over the coming days and weeks:

- When you were little and playing "pretend", what did you pretend to be?

- What memories do you have of childhood? What are the common themes? What role do you play in each? What strengths do you perceive?

- When you were in high school, what career path did you see for yourself? What did you dream of doing?

- When you daydream, what are your fantasies? Who are you? What are you doing? Who are you with?

(continued on next page)

38

- Imagine you are walking down the street and you see yourself approaching. This version of you has completed this midlife transition. What is different about her? Start a dialogue. What do you need to know? What does she have to say?

- Start a journal entry with the words "I give you permission to....".

- Picture yourself at about age five. Find a happy moment. Now, have that five-year-old compose a letter to you.

Notes:

Notes:

Notes:

Notes:

Chapter 3

Reintegration and Reinvention

"Life shrinks or expands in proportion to one's courage."
—Anais Nin

By the time you get to about age 50, chances are you'll be more content with yourself and more fulfilled in your life. How do I know? Well, I've got a lot of faith in this program, I've got a lot of faith in womankind and, I've also got some pretty good predictive data. A book published by the National Association of Social Workers (in America) reported that nearly half of all the women aged 51 that it surveyed reported high levels of personal achievement and a newfound sense of adventure.

Furthermore, Australian scholars Ailsa Burns and Rosemary Leonard found, after conducting life-review interviews with 60 women, that the most important "turning points" in these women's lives were not menopause or the empty nest, but rather personal-growth experiences. In other words, they were most marked by changes that started from within. Burns and Leonard found that the orientation inward, toward self-transcendence, versus outward, toward the external world, were most significant, particularly for women in the second half of life.

For the majority of women who have navigated the midlife transition, an enhanced awareness and acceptance of self has lead to an enhanced experience of life. Sounds pretty good, doesn't it?

So, how do you get there? Well, you're on your way. You're paying attention to your feelings, you're solidifying your self-concept, you're revisiting your past for clues to missing pieces of yourself. And now, in the final stages of your journey, you'll need to integrate all of that and see where it takes you.

Janet, at 44, left a verbally and emotionally abusive marriage, turned her back on her career as a lawyer and embarked on a degree in divinity; she intends to enter pastoral duties in the coming year.

Wanda was a judge. But she loved singing. She resigned her seat on the bench to work part-time as a lawyer so she could devote more of her time to writing and recording music.

Mary was a pharmacist with a passion for plants and flowers. She retrained so that she could head up a naturopathic division at her pharmacy.

Anna decided that, after taking time away from a veterinary career to birth two babies, she didn't really want to go back to veterinary work. Her passion was photography. She took a series of courses and began a freelance career as an animal and child portrait photographer.

Fiorella found she was enjoying her time in the kitchen far more than the time she spent in her office. When she was (conveniently) downsized just after her 41st birthday, she dug into her family's rich Italian culinary heritage and published a cookbook. She now teaches cooking classes, leads workshops and develops recipes.

In their study, published in 2007 in *Menopause: The Journal of the North American Menopause Society,* researchers Beyene, Gilliss and Lee conducted in-depth interviews with 53 premenopausal women ranging in age from 40 to 48. Of the main themes that emerged from the interviews, these are of particular note: the women expressed a renewed focus on the self; and most were reassessing goals and options for the future. Self-growth and new opportunities marked the journey of these women as they made their way through midlife.

Four midlife healthcare professionals at the University of Victoria in British Columbia, Canada, put their own lives under the microscope to come up with the major issues that define a woman's midlife experience. Marla Arvay, Elizabeth Banister, Mary Hoskins and Anita Snell explored the concept of "self" at midlife. One of the dominant plotlines that emerged was the striving for authenticity—a desire for a woman to be her "true" self and not just the self she is expected to be, or has been socialized to be. "Who is it possible for me to be, who do I truly want to be, when I'm not playing proscribed roles?" A deepened and enriched sense of inner knowing—what one study participant described as "an ancient, inner, quiet thing" —characterized the midlife experience of these women. Indeed, many midlife women feel they emerge from the transitory tunnel with a heightened sense of consciousness, with a transcendent self (one that is more spiritual and wise) and with a new clarity about themselves and others.

But what's more, these researchers put words to what many women at midlife feel: the need to evolve. There is a strong compulsion to morph, to move, to change. Perhaps because we are at the midway point of our lives with the disconcerting feeling that half of our time is in the rear-view mirror, many forty-something women begin to embrace a sort of spiritual Darwinism: an urge toward psychic adaptation, an evolved identity.

48

It isn't so much that our past lives have been a fraud, but rather that they no longer feel right. For many of my clients, the midlife malaise is about wearing a life that no longer fits—it's a discomfort that comes from being forced to live in a way that no longer feels authentic, that is too small and constraining, that feels like a prison and leaves a woman yearning for the freedom to be more fully herself and do what she truly wants to do.

That freedom comes from honouring this new self, and also from shedding preassigned roles and preconceived rules. It's time to get naked. Strip away all of the roles you play—mother, sister, caregiver, partner, community leader, volunteer. These are just things you do; they are not who you are. Many of us fall into the trap of defining ourselves by what we do. So, when we are no longer happy with the things we do (the roles we play) then, by extension, we are not happy with our very selves.

It's important to separate who we are from what we do. What we do is changeable—we can always do differently. And what about who we are? Is that changeable too? Buddhists believes that the notion of "self" is a distraction, an illusion. By preoccupying ourselves with questions of self and others—Who am I? Who are they? What is mine? What is theirs?—we are not considering more expansive question and are not practicing more expansive strategies. Namely, we are not training the mind toward virtue, concentration and calm. In essence, we become selfish at the expense of enlightenment.

What if we were to let go of our dependency on roles and identity and see self not as something we have but as something we do? In essence, then, we are "selfing" every day; each moment is an opportunity to create, or manifest, who we want to be. In each moment we can ask ourselves if we want to give, or if we want to receive, if we want to be empathetic or if we want to be detached.

The great Austrian theorist (founder of the school of individual psychology) Alfred Adler reminded us that we are both the artist and the canvas. We create ourselves. Developing such a conceptualization of self that is fluid and not static is ultimately liberating, especially now, at midlife.

So, who do you want to be? Let's start putting all of this together. In chapters one and two of this book you found anchors—core traits that underpin your personhood. If we truly embrace those traits—really own them—then we find ourselves in a position of choice: Which of these traits do I want to come out to play? And when and how? What a wonderful vantage point from which to view the next phase of life!

Now, if you are one of those people who find complete liberation utterly paralyzing, that's OK. The notion of a blank canvas can be daunting. But keep in mind, the palette has been pre-selected and it's right at hand. So, if you don't yet have a clear picture, don't worry. Let's break it down even further. Here's what I want you to do:

- Imagine for a minute that money is no object.

- Just for a second, strip away the roles of mother, caregiver, partner, employee of the month—whatever roles currently define you. You don't have to discard them completely, but for now you're just going to put them aside.

- Now, revisit the core traits and strengths that you revealed in Chapter 1. What are the attributes you most cherish about yourself?

- Consider the dreams and plans you had in childhood and adolescence. Which ones still light you up?

- Ask yourself again: What do I now want my life to look like? What do I need to change in order to bring my life in line with who I truly am and what I truly want in life?

Still not sure where you need to go and what you need to do? Let's dig down a little deeper.

Zeroing In

So, where do you start? You probably have some idea of the area of your life that feels most out of sync. But if you don't (well, even if you do), try this exercise, created by Susan Pye Brokaw, psychotherapist and core faculty member at the Adler Graduate School in Minnesota. Draw a large circle on a piece of paper. Divide the circle into five equal parts, as if you were drawing a pie with five slices. Now, label each section as follows: put "love and sex" in one slice, "friends" in the second, "work" in the third, "self" in the fourth, and "spirituality" in the fifth.

Physician and psychotherapist Alfred Adler argued that all of the challenges we face in life fall into these critical areas. As we evolve and grow, our goal is to overcome perceived or real inferiorities and learn to cooperate with others in order to find solutions to these "tasks of life." Typically, we struggle more in one area than the others. So, I want you to go around the circle rating your happiness in each area. On a scale of 1 to 10, with 1 being as low as you can go and 10 representing perfection, rate how you feel about your life in each of the areas. Now, take a look at your wheel of life. Any surprises? Here's what we look for: any section that rates under about a 7. I don't expect to see 10s—that represents perfection, which is an impossible ideal. But 7s and 8s are realistic goals.

Anything less than 7, though, signals an area of your life in need of some work, whether a minor renovation or a major reconstruction. Focus your efforts and insights there.

$\mathcal{A}$voiding Stumbling Blocks

As we motor through our lives, it's important to know what's driving us. What is filling our subconscious fuel tank? What are our hidden, yet powerful, motivating forces? Within each of us lie a bunch of buried beliefs—perceptions about what is good and what is bad, what we should seek and what we should evade. These perceptions are formed early in life and become a sort of psychic GPS system. Among those beliefs there's one that is particularly powerful: our deepest fear. At some point in our childhood each of us experienced or witnessed something that made us think, "*That*, above all else, must be avoided at all costs."

In our effort to avoid *that-which-is-most-painful-or-worrying* we develop clever coping strategies. Those coping mechanisms help us maneuver around our mental minefields, those trouble spots. And that's not necessarily a bad thing—if we are conscious of what's in our fuel tank and have our hands securely on the wheel! The trouble is, if we aren't aware of our hidden driving forces, it's like we have our foot on the accelerator but our hands aren't on the wheel. We have blind spots. We don't act, we react. And we get tripped up or detoured. We wind up in the same dead ends and we aren't clear how we got there.

So, since we're here anyway, enjoying this little pause at the midway point of our lives, let's take the blinders off once and for all. What is your biggest stumbling block? In my experience, the women who experience the greatest existential angst at midlife have one of two main emotional priorities. These women fall into one of two camps:

1. Those who seek to avoid Meaninglessness or Unimportance

- Your greatest dread is a life devoid of meaning, or to have relationships that aren't imbued with meaning. To be considered unimportant, or to lead a life that is unimportant, is a fate worse than death.

- You achieve your goal (of avoiding any whiff of meaninglessness or unimportance) by striving for superiority. Being "best"—whether better than all the others, or the best possible version of yourself you can possibly be—offers you a guarantee against mediocrity. For you, there is no such thing as "good enough." You constantly strive for better, better, best; to be better than you are; to be top of the heap.

- Your nutshell belief: "If I'm not the best, I'm not enough." Or, "If I'm not the top dog, I'm the bottom of the barrel."

- Your greatest gift to the planet, your family and yourself is that you encourage others to want more, do more, be more. You are the wind beneath the wings of many around you. Your striving spirit is a driving force for the people who count on you.

- The price you pay is the price of perfection. Your bar is set so high that you feel you are constantly failing to achieve enough, to do enough. And, since staying on top is such a high priority, you may find yourself averse to risks (that could topple you) or you may become stuck on a hamster wheel, unable to give up your race to supremacy. You may have lost sight of your joy in your relentless pursuit of mastery.

- The price those around you pay is exclusion. It's lonely at the top. Being above others means that at times you are not amongst them. Sometimes your superior striving spirit leaves others in your dust. They may also feel intimidated, as your ferocious drive is read by others as arrogance and that may cost you intimacy.

- Your action plan is to give yourself permission to get off the hamster wheel. (You must be exhausted!) That yearning to better-better-best can act like blinders—you're so focused on achieving higher and higher heights that you aren't enjoying the view. You've completely lost sight of your joy. What would you choose to do if you weren't so worried about best-ness? What detours are you refusing to consider? What rest stops might appeal if you allowed yourself a break? What would your life look like if you decided that instead of being perfect, you were going to be perfectly happy? What if instead of focusing on being the best you focused on finding the best fit?

2. Those who seek to avoid Rejection

- Your greatest dread is to be left out, to be excluded or to be unwanted. The worry that others won't want you is the undercurrent in all of your relationships.

- You achieve your goal (of avoiding rejection) by pleasing others. You are an expert at not only putting others before yourself, but also morphing to be what you believe they want or need you to be.

- Your greatest gift is your empathy. Your ability to read others has become so honed that no one can beat you for compassion and caring.

- The price you pay is, well, a sense of self. You have spent so long pleasing others that you've forgotten what it is that you want, what pleases you. You measure your worth by your success at doing for others. When was the last time you put yourself first? If you're feeling lost at midlife, it may be that you have temporarily lost sight of your soul.

- The price others pay is a sense of authenticity. Since you are so good at playing the chameleon, they are forced to forfeit knowing the genuine you. Your pleasing nature makes you an easy person to get along with, but at times the camouflage you wear creates a disconnect —it's part and parcel of wearing that disguise.

Ask yourself: If a miracle happened overnight and you awoke to a world in which you were no longer stressed, exhausted or depressed, how would you know? Picture yourself getting out of bed. What's the first thing you notice? What's different? The answer to this question reveals one major change you can make now to benefit the rest of your life.

- Your action plan is to start tapping into what truly makes you tick. What lights you up? I bet you aren't really sure. So, pretend, just for a second, that you weren't afraid of what others might think. Imagine, just for a second, that you were worthy without earning their indebtedness. If you gave yourself permission to take off your camouflage gear and assert yourself, what would you ask for? Put yourself out there. Experiment with saying no, with speaking up. Do others really think less of you? Do they leave you? Probably not. So, start tapping into your joy now. When do you feel most alive?

$\mathcal{P}$laying Pretend

OK so you've narrowed down the possibilities and removed the stumbling blocks. Now what? Sometimes, the best way to find out if something fits is to try it on for size. You wouldn't buy a new car without taking it out for a test drive; you wouldn't buy a new suit without first making sure it fit. In this exercise, you're going to try on a new you.

Before you begin, make a shortlist of the new roles, jobs or changes you believe feel the most right for you right now. Maybe you're thinking of ditching city life for a place in the country, or moving to the coast. Maybe you're pondering a new profession, or going half-time to invest more time on your passion. What have you been musing on since starting this book? Whether it's a new career or a new kayak, write it down.

Now, choose one that you'd be willing to try on for a week. For the next seven days, act as if you have made that change. Pay attention to how you feel. Are you energized, enlightened, relieved? Or worried, bored or drained? Make notes.

But wait, we're not done yet. Choose another item from your list. Act as if you've made that change and make note of your feelings again. Repeat this exercise until you've exhausted your list.

Which "outfit" did you dread taking off? Which one did you jump out of bed dying to put back on? You've found your answer. Now, all you need is to leap.

And this is where you'll need to call upon your courage. Interestingly, the word courage comes from the Latin word "cor," or heart. So, really, having courage isn't so much about having guts as it is having heart. Courage is about listening to our heartfelt feelings. It's about being true to those feelings. True to our deepest selves. And sure, sometimes that takes bravery.

All brave acts start with single steps. You've already taken one—you read this book. What's next? That part is up to you.

Summary of Key Points:

- Changes from within can be turning points; research suggests that more than 50 percent of women become happier and more content in the second half of their lives.

- The push to the finish line involves integrating your core strengths and your true desires in a way that strives for authenticity.

- Enhanced awareness and acceptance of self can lead to enhanced experience of life.

- We need to be courageous enough to shed pre-assigned roles and preconceived rules; many women at midlife feel the need for self-growth, spiritual evolution that honour our cores and builds out from them.

- In order to do so we need to discover our stumbling blocks: a fear of meaninglessness? Of rejection?

- Consider the notion that we create ourselves; Each moment is an opportunity to create or manifest who we want to be.

- Brave acts start with single steps; find the courage to take one step at a time.

Notes:

Notes:

Notes:

Notes:

Conclusion

You're probably wondering what happened to that woman in the canoe—that sad, stuck version of myself. Well, she eventually put her paddle in and committed herself to a new direction. She decided to forgo the usual destination—that rocky outcropping that had been her traditional stopping place. Instead, after having a good cry, she paddled aimlessly for awhile. She scouted the banks and got comfortable not knowing exactly where she was headed.

If you're anything like me, not having a goal is tantamount to torture. Getting Zen about the journey and not obsessing about the destination was challenging for me. I had to rewire my thinking: rejecting old goals and being open to new ones was the goal. Emptying my psychic space to make room for new world views, new versions of myself, new dreams—that was the aim. And that required me to get comfy in limbo. Just for a time. I had to be OK with being lost in order to be found.

And I did. I found myself. I found a version of me that was more than I had been before. It was a rounder, fuller personhood—one that integrated pieces of my lost little girl, one that honoured my deepest truths. I put my paddle in and pointed my bow toward a new purpose. I made it through the valley of midlife (or the dark wood of Dante's and Jung's middle-aged depictions).

To quote, again, author and poet David Whyte, "We take the road of midlife not as the beginning of disengagement and retirement but as a newer and profounder path to meaningful work, the work of belonging in a deeper way to those people and things we have learned to love. The task of midlife is the task of finding the difficult, often dangerous road to this eldership of love. It becomes, for all of us, the road worth taking, the road back home."

"Home" is a place deep inside ourselves. It's a place where we know our worthiness, where our strengths aren't filtered through self-doubts. It's a place of joy and non-judgment. It's a place of peace and purpose. It's a place of humility and humour. It's a place of wisdom and whimsy. And only you know how to find it. The road map is in your hands. And the highway beckons. Bon voyage!

$\mathcal{S}$ummary of Key Points:

- Rejecting old goals and being open to new ones is critical.

- It's helpful to get Zen about the journey, trusting that the destination will become clear.

- Make room for new world views, new versions of self, new dreams.

Notes:

Notes:

Notes:

Notes:

Author Biography

Photograph taken by
Naomi Finlay

Liza Finlay is a registered psychotherapist with a private practice in Toronto, Canada. She gives speeches and workshops at conferences and colleges and major corporations. She teaches at the Adler Graduate School in Richfield, Minnesota. Before beginning her psychotherapy practice, Liza spent two decades as a magazine feature writer, authoring mental health articles for some of Canada's biggest titles. She lives in Toronto with all "her boys"—her husband, two sons, and two male dogs.

CPSIA information can be obtained
at www.ICGtesting.com
Printed in the USA
LVHW092006030519
616638LV00001B/26/P